Prentice-Hall, Inc., Englewood Cliffs, New Jersey 07632

How to Live with a Headstrong Horse

Eric Gurney

Library of Congress Cataloging in Publication Data

Gurney, Eric.
  How to live with a headstrong horse.

1. Horses—Caricatures and cartoons.   2. American
wit and humor, Pictorial.   I. Title.
NC1429.G87A4 1983   741.5'973   82-19708
ISBN 0-13-415406-1

This book is available at a special discount when ordered
in bulk quantities. Contact Prentice-Hall, Inc.,
General Publishing Division, Special Sales, Englewood Cliffs, N. J. 07632

10   9   8   7   6   5   4   3   2   1

Printed in the United States of America

Production editor: Marlys Lehmann
Manufacturing buyer: Patrick Mahoney

ISBN 0-13-415406-1

Prentice-Hall International, Inc., *London*
Prentice-Hall of Australia Pty. Limited, *Sydney*
Prentice-Hall of Canada Inc., *Toronto*
Prentice-Hall of India Private Limited, *New Delhi*
Prentice-Hall of Japan, Inc., *Tokyo*
Prentice-Hall of Southeast Asia Pte. Ltd., *Singapore*
Whitehall Books Limited, *Wellington, New Zealand*
Editora Prentice-Hall do Brasil Ltda., *Rio de Janeiro*

DEDICATED TO
NANCY PREVO
FOR
HER HELP
AND INSPIRATION

Contents

The dawn horse could have ridden man,
had man been around at that time.

1

The Headstrong Horse
Through History

Many, many years before man and woman arrived on the scene the horse was roaming the earth munching on the lushest and tastiest bits of vegetation he could find. This he well needed because at that time, he was no bigger than a fox terrier. In Latin, he was called *Eohippus,* or in the language of the layman, he was known as the Dawn Horse. Because he was not then the speedy steed he is today, he was forced to hide in the bountiful forests to keep from being an after-dinner snack for some of the huge monsters that were constantly on the lookout for just such tasty targets. A few million years rolled by before the stature of the horse changed. As the forests thinned out the Great Plains became larger and places to hide became as scarce as hair on a billiard ball, so the horse had to run for his life. His legs grew longer, and he changed from leaf-eater to grass-consumer. After about fifty million years of various developing, he became large enough for the use of man.

At first, men hunted the horse for food until someone with a sharp mind and a lazy body had the brilliant idea of using the horse for transportation. Most of this story happened right here on the American continent. When Columbus discovered North America in 1492, the horses were long gone. Where had they disappeared to? No one really knows. In 1518, shortly after

Columbus, Don Hernando Cortes came to America and re-introduced the horse to this continent. There were sixteen of them to be exact. He was followed by Hernando de Soto who brought 250 horses. This all happened before the discovery of the seasick pill, so you can imagine the disheveled-looking groups that disembarked onto the shores of America.

The Indians' hair stood on end when they first saw horse and man together. They immediately fled in terror of what they thought was a half man and half beast. Later, when they caught on to the real facts and saw what a wonderful asset it was to own such a magnificent and useful creature, they began stealing horses from the Spaniards. After that, it became even more of a challenge for the Indians to steal horses from each other, especially on moonless nights.

"What a ham!"

1 Man's first...

2   attempt...

3   to ride a horse . . .

4   must have been...

5   a wild one...

6   in more...

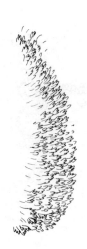

7   ways...

8   than...

9   ....

10   ...one.

Stealing horses from the Spaniards was heap big fun,

but horse lifting from each other...

was even more of a challenge.

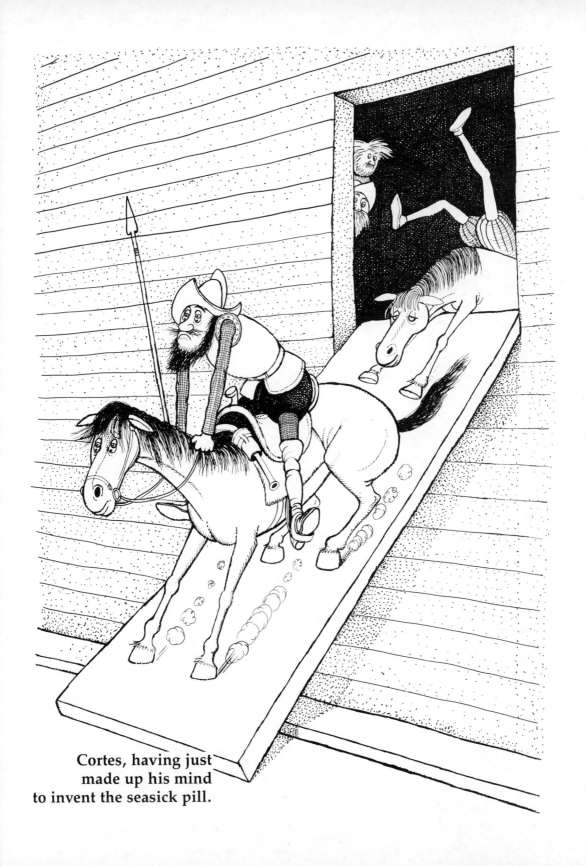

Cortes, having just
made up his mind
to invent the seasick pill.

Horse Breeds

THE THOROUGHBRED

The Thoroughbred can cause one either to bring home a wheelbarrowfull of money, or to lose one's shirt at the races and come home wearing a barrel.

The Thoroughbred is the great breed known as the racehorse, and was developed by some astute English horse-breeders with an eye for making money in the early eighteenth century. Three Arabian stallions were imported and bred to some bigger English mares whose offspring maintained most of the Arabian traits. Their speed was intensified and they had gained nearly an inch in height. Each following generation gained in height, size, and speed. By the year 1850, they had made the original Arabians look as if they were being viewed through the wrong ends of binoculars. They then stood a good six inches taller than the original Arabian stallions. They had longer legs and could bluestreak around a racetrack faster than you can say "a horse of a different color"! In fact, they could do a mile in less than two minutes. Today, the lines of a Thoroughbred still trace back to any one of the three Arabian stallions. He is now the swiftest in distance of all the equine breeds and his efforts on the race track make up the "Sport of Kings."

THE ARABIAN

If an equestrian wants to own the oldest and purest breed of horse that money can buy, he should loosen up his purse strings, let the moths fly out and buy himself a beautiful, intelligent, people-loving Arabian horse. Where it originated nobody seems to know but we do know it was carefully bred in ancient Arabia. It seems strange that in a desert country as unfriendly to the needs of the horse as a swarm of killer bees, there should develop a type of horse with such speed and stamina. The Arabian horse is so well loved in the United States that there are more of them living here than in all of Saudi Arabia, Turkey, Syria, Iraq, Iran, Jordan, Pakistan, and India combined.

The Arabian horse came to India around 1290 as a result of a shipwreck.

The American Quarterhorse

THE AMERICAN QUARTERHORSE

For one quarter of a mile the American Quarterhorse can run faster than a spider with a match under it. Hence his name the Quarterhorse. In fact, he can outdistance any horse. In the early days of Virginia the colonists wanted a horse that would do double duty, one that could farm the land and also be used after a day's work in their favorite sport—match racing. The Colonists bred Spanish Jennets to English Pacers and the American Quarterhorse came to be. But as everyone loves a winner, he became second best when the English Thoroughbred was imported. He might have been completely forgotten if he had not made the trip to the new western frontiers. There, the Quarterhorse was like manna from heaven for the cowboys. He could round up cattle, climb mountains like a mountain goat, swim streams like Tarzan, and cut a steer out of the herd better than a motorcycle, helicopter, or any other machine invented since. Not only that, but he knew just what to do when the cowboy's lariat tightened over the neck of a steer. He would slide to a stop and brace himself against the bucking, bellowing bovine. Along with all these wonderful qualities the Quarterhorse had a friendly, stable nature. He was a cowboy's best friend and could twirl around so fast that he would make a whirling dervish look as if he were stuck in the mud. As a result he became a crackerjack polo pony.

THE APPALOOSA

The Appaloosa horse is the delight of the cowboy- and- Indian artists, and also the frustrated interior- and- exterior decorators who have a regular field day polkadotting everything in sight. These unique markings were developed by horse breeders in the Palouse Valley in the Northwest section of America and were carefully bred by the Nez Perce Indians who only bred the best to the best to get the specific coat patterns referred to as "blankets." The Appaloosa's great-grandparents were descendants of the horses brought over by the Conquistadores of Spain during the sixteenth century. Because of his remarkable design, coloring, and talent, he is popular in circuses, parades, gymkanas, rodeos, horse shows, and on ranches.

The Appaloosa

THE CLYDESDALE

The Clydesdale does his fancy stepping by the bonnie banks of the Clyde River in Scotland and is the pride of the Scottish people. He is the most stylish of the big four—the Belgians, the Percherons, the Shires, and the Clydesdales. His high-stepping walk makes him appear to be enjoying whatever he is doing, even if it is pulling a load of manure. In America, he has gained a great reputation as the exciting eight-horse team that pulls the Budweiser beer wagon and appears at rodeos, parades, and on TV commercials.

The Clydesdale

The Clydesdale originally was used as a farm horse and for transporting coal from the Scottish mines. Contests are held to determine which horse will plow a furrow as straight as William Tell's arrow enroute to the apple on top of his son's head, and nearly as fast!

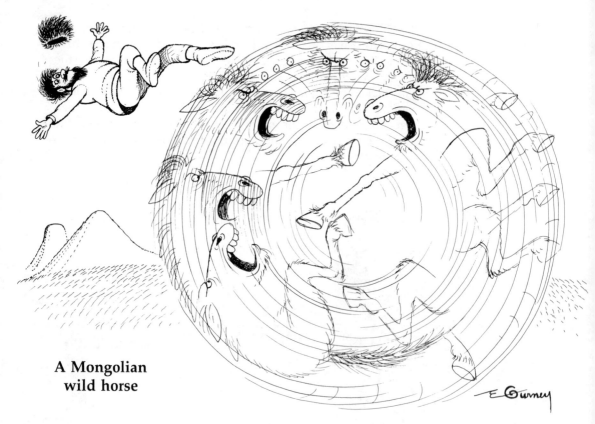

**A Mongolian
wild horse**

**If you can't pronounce
Przewalski just call it a Mongolian wild horse.**

THE PRZEWALSKI or Mongolian Wild Horse

If you are not Russian and have a tough time pronouncing the word Przewalski, just call him a Mongolian Wild Horse. He was discovered in 1881 by a Russian explorer who was sashaying around the area of the Tachin Schara Nuru Mountains which are situated at the western edge of the Gobi Desert. The extreme hot and cold climate in this area is one of the most revolting you can imagine, but this situation does not seem to faze this independent animal one iota. He is endowed with great powers of endurance and is able to exist on the most miserable and sparse vegetation Mongolia has to offer.

THE SHETLAND PONY

The Shetland Pony came from the wilds of the Shetland Islands situated about 150 kilometers (100 miles) off the north coast of Scotland where the cold wind blows hard enough to turn one's nose a beautiful turquoise blue in five seconds flat. As a result of such tough weather conditions these ponies have become very rugged and hardy. They were originally used for such jobs as packing peat moss and hauling coal carts in the mines.

Since nearly all the coal mines and farms are now mechanized, the ponies have become wonderful pets and companions for small children who like to pretend they are a popular cowboy star, or the winning jockey of the Kentucky Derby.

The Shetland pony is the smallest of all Britain's nine native breeds.

THE MORGAN HORSE

Justin Morgan, a singing teacher, made plenty of nothing in the money department, but became world famous because of his horse. He and his small bay stallion spent hours traveling the twisting, hilly Vermont roads going from school to school teaching singing. The horse was thought to be of Thoroughbred and Arab extraction with a little Welsh blood thrown in for good measure. Only when the horse was long gone was its true worth understood. Horse people were amazed that its offspring were exact duplicates in looks, courage, strength, and willingness to work. Suddenly it all rang a bell. They realized that that single horse had founded a whole new breed. The breed was named Justin Morgan after the singing teacher. The Morgan horse was used to haul logs, plow fields, and do all kinds of chores. On Sundays it would be groomed and with its harness brasses polished and head held high it would take the family to church.

**The Morgan horse was named after his owner,
a pennyless singing teacher, Justin Morgan.**

Leaping Lippizaners should look before they leap.

THE LIPIZZANER

You would think it had four pogo sticks attached to its legs when it performs its sensational leaps. Because of this, this Austrian horse is one of the most celebrated in the world.

When Lipizzaners are born, they are as black as India ink and become lighter with age until their coats are as white as Santa Claus's beard. This whiteness makes them quite spectacular when they perform their famous ballet with graceful pirouettes and giant leaps into space.

In the year 1480, the breed we know as the Lipizzaner was created by the emissary of Archduke Charles, the Freiherr von Khevenhiller, using nine amorous stallions and twenty-four willing mares from Spain. This emissary, the Spanish Riding School of Vienna, and the Lipizzaner together have made each other famous. It is not uncommon for some of these horses to perform their routines until the age of thirty because of the excellent care they receive. Or is it because they don't know how old they really are?

Some people are inclined to pamper their horses.

Care of the
Headstrong Horse

Your horse enjoys being babied and fussed over just as much as the rest of us.

Bathing a horse naturally takes one a little longer than bathing a wire-haired terrier and for those who can afford it, there are all kinds of dog salons where you can take your dog to be bathed, its hair and whiskers to be trimmed and its nails to be manicured. Unfortunately, there are no salons for horses. Years ago when the horse used to furnish most of the power for transportation, a lot of the considerate drivers would shelter their horses' heads from the summer sun with an old discarded hat, and in the cold months they would invest in a horse blanket for warmth. As a result, some of those horses looked as if they were on their way to a masquerade ball.

**If your horse is used to eating at the stroke of 12 noon,
don't be an idiot and take him riding at that time.**

Be sure to keep his stable freshly painted.

1   Your horse will appreciate...

2   his brand new wool coat...

3   almost as much as...

4   the moths.

1

2

3

4

5

6

7

8

Makeshift shoeing will look pretty jazzy, but it is
not very utilitarian, especially for a working horse.

If old Ramble doesn't
like a cold hose shower,
you may end up getting it.

1 Most horses...

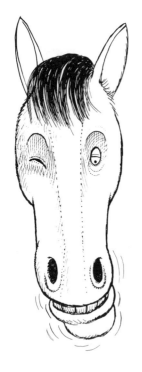

2 are...   3 endowed...

4   with . . .

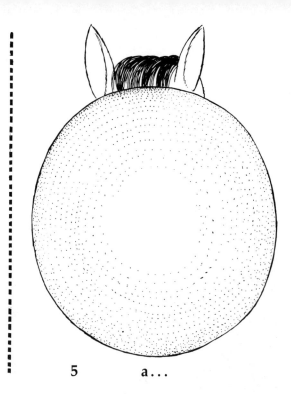

5   a . . .

6   bit of . . .

7   a sweet tooth.

1

If you ever become forgetful...

2

some horses will jog...

3

your memory for you.

HEADWEAR

Rain

For the hot sun

The junkman's horse

The chimney sweep's horse

Circus parade

The Chinese influence

Variety...

1

in their
feeding habits...

2

is the spice
of life.

3

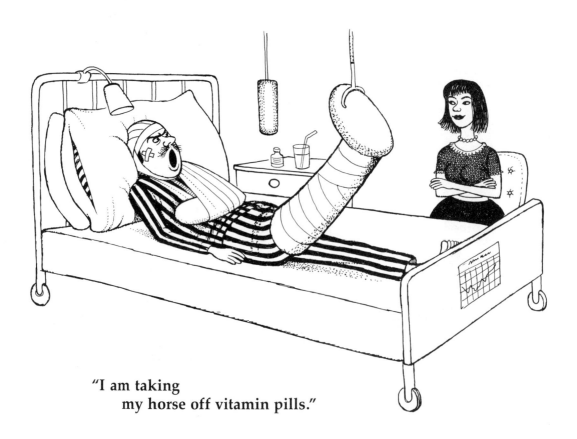

"I am taking
  my horse off vitamin pills."

The first and last
customer of the day.

Training your horse
to swim is a good way
to get rid of horse flies.

Training the Headstrong Horse

To train a horse properly, one has to have the patience of Job, the calmness of a tightrope walker and the disposition of a saint. If a trainer is neurotic, his or her horse will end up as jumpy as a runaway flea on a hot tin roof during a heat wave. Since the horse is quite a simple soul, the trainer should use the absolutely simplest terms in his or her lessons.

A well-trained horse should be a real pleasure to ride no matter what pursuit it is involved in and at the same time be a very happy and contented animal. The variety of endeavors that horses have learned to cope with is amazing. He may not be able to beat you at checkers, but he can second guess the next move of a maverick steer and cut the steer out of the main herd any time.

1   You should set your horse a good example.   One...

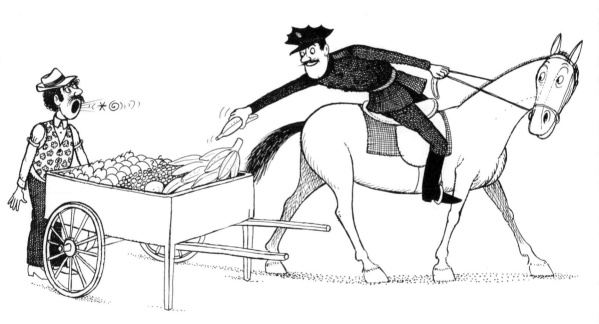

2   bad turn...

3   deserves...

4   another.

1

2

3

4

5

Don't change horses in midstream.

5

Horse Quotations

In the year 1855, a man by the name of John Bartlett created a book of all the well-known quotations he could lay his hands on. The original book was put together without any thought of publication. Later on he decided it would be a great idea to publish it, which he then did himself after he had enlarged his first collection. It was such a success that during his life he edited nine more editions. I can imagine John Bartlett, up to his armpits in thousands of books and magazines, putting together this fabulous collection of quotes. With many thanks to John Bartlett, here are a few of them:

My kingdom for a horse!

You can lead a horse to water, but you can't make him drink.

Don't change horses in midstream.

Don't look a gift horse in the mouth.

A horse of a different color...

You nailed the horseshoe upside down...

Don't put the cart before the horse.

The best of luck is always waiting on you
if you pick up on the road a horse's shoe.

Pride goeth before a fall.

For want of a nail the shoe is lost,
For want of a shoe the horse is lost,
For want of a horse the rider is lost.

Don't look
a gift horse
in the mouth.

A horse of
a different color...

No wonder skies
upon you frown...

You nailed
the horseshoe
upside down...

Just turn it 'round
and you will see...

How you and fortune...   will agree.

1   Pride goeth...

2   before...

3   a...

4   fall.

Race horses love to have a mascot.

Horse Sports

The first form of sport with man and horse collaborating was the four-horse chariot race, held as early as the twenty-third Olympiad (688 B.C.) in Greece. There were as many as forty chariots competing in this wild rush to win a pot of gold. About fifty years later, mule races were introduced at which the roaring crowd could wildly cheer their favorite mule to victory.

A few centuries later the Romans took up the sport with typical Italian gusto and held as many as twenty-four races a day. It was the Romans who introduced the horse race into not-too-jolly old Britain at the time. But the Christian church frowned on the early horse races since fun, to the Puritans, was something wicked and an invention of the Devil himself. However, racing continued to flourish and Charles the Second made Newmarket the headquarters of the turf in Britain. Since then the art of fox hunting, trotting, polo, and stadium and cross-country jumping have increased by leaps and bounds.

Please don't ask
what he is going to do
for an encore.

"If you can't lick 'em, by all means join 'em."

However, there are always exceptions.

An almost certain goal

is saved.

**If you're going to the masquerade ball
dressed as a horse, be sure you're not in the hind end....**

The front end has all the fun.

An Eastern dude, as seen by his rented Western horse.

The Headstrong Western Horse

The Mustang was a descendant from the early Spanish horses brought to America by Cortes. After a few centuries of every horse for itself in the breeding department, horses became hammer-headed, ewe necked, sway backed, and cow hocked. One will never see this pictured in the glamorized paintings by some of the cowboy artists of today.

The Indians became expert in the art of riding and could zip around a buffalo like a bumblebee around a flower at the same time filling the buffalo full of arrows. This meant lots of goodies in the wigwam culinary department.

The Mustang became a natural cow pony and could carry his cowboy safely around the savage longhorn cattle that were capable of killing a man on foot. There were all kinds of other Western riders using the Mustang. Trappers, miners, hunters, prospectors, and most famous of all, the Pony Express riders, depended upon this intrepid beast. "T'ain't a fit night for man nor beast" never stopped these horses and riders from their appointed rounds.

1

2

3

1   Who needs a fast trip to the local saloon...

2   when right nearby is...

3

a nibble of...

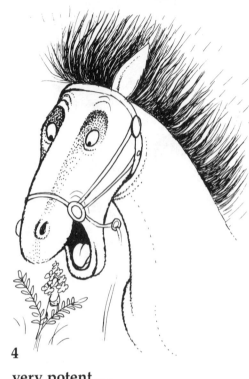

4

very potent...

5

locoweed?

6

7

8

1   "It's...

2   an...

3   ill...

4   wind...

5   that...

6   doesn't...

7   blow...

8   someone...

9

10   some...

11

12   ...good.

American horses learned to buck when attacked

by vicious wild cats.

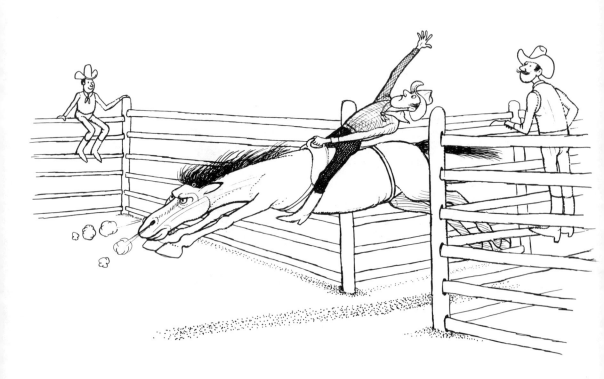

1   When a killer bronco...

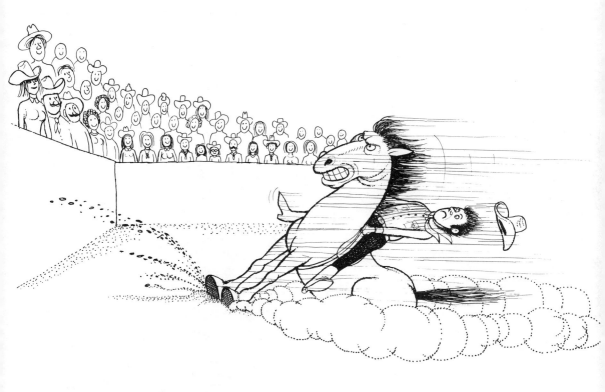

2   suddenly...

3   turns soft,

4   your act has had it.

The Pony Express

8

The Headstrong
Working Horse

As most of the sources of information on the history of employment for the horse are about as vague as a ship seen in the Newfoundland fog banks, I will have to take a wild guess at the first working task given to the horse and that that horse was a pack animal. Even today in America, especially in the mountain regions, the pack horse is still put to good use. As the proper horse collar had not been developed in ancient times, man had to rely on a clumsy yoke- and- strap system. As a result, it meant using far more horses than were necessary. For instance, in the Roman chariot races, four horses were used, while today we see only one in harness at the races. After the invention of the horse collar, horses were used to perform more jobs than there are beads on an Indian moccasin. There were jobs on farms, horse-drawn barges and trams, roundups of cattle, stage coaches to be pulled, and even rounds with the milk wagons. Some of these horses knew the routes, the customer stops, and the bars with the best spirits better than the milkman himself did. Performing circus horses seem more to play than to work as they carry everything from acrobats to dogs on their backs as they lope at a steady pace around the ring.

In American history, the Pony Express, and the hundreds of other uses performed by the horse, made the development of the West possible.

1

2

3

4

Cutting out a steer could look like

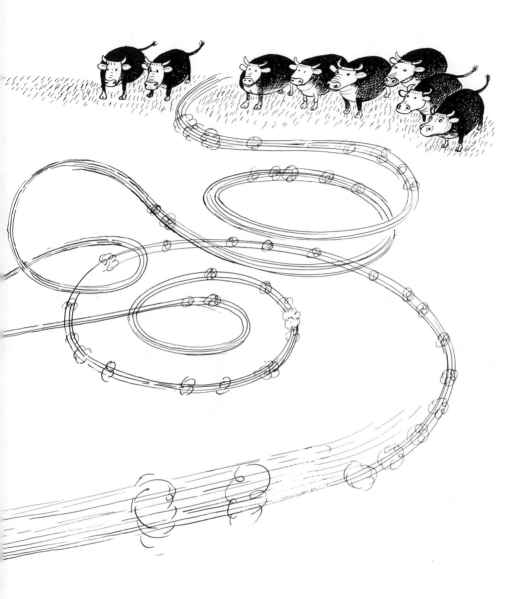

the flight pattern of a hummingbird.

In some countries horses are
still indispensable for rounding up sheep.

**Working horses
need sweets for energy.**

Keeping the soldiers quiet inside
the Trojan horse was
at times most difficult.

Famous
Headstrong Horses

THE TROJAN HORSE

One of the best known horses of all time was the famous Greek
wooden horse called the Trojan Horse. The inspiration for the
idea of building a huge wooden horse came from a wily old coot
named Prylis. The Trojan horse held twenty-five armed men
inside it and was, supposedly, an offering to the goddess,
Athene. Prylis knew that the fancy footwork boys amongst the
Trojans could not resist stealing the horse and taking it into their
walled-in city. Then, when night fell and all were asleep, Prylis
planned to have the Greek soldiers inside spring through the
trap door of the horse and destroy the unsuspecting city. His
plan almost failed when an intrepid Trojan warrior jammed his
spear up through the belly of the wooden horse, grazing one of
the soldiers who, fortunately, kept his cool and remained silent,
thus saving all their lives. The plan worked perfectly and it was
the turning point of the war in favor of the Greeks.

It's up, up, and away for Don Quixote while Rosinante watches.

ROSINANTE

They say love is blind, and it certainly was in the case of Don Quixote, who saw in his raw-boned, scrawny, elderly horse nothing but beauty and nobility. He pictured himself and Rosinante as the absolute crème de la crème. Rosinante didn't really want to do anything but stay home and quietly eat grass, but Don Quixote had other plans. He wanted to attack and conquer windmills, which he pictured as revolting and revolving giants. Unfortunately, his first charge backfired when a sudden gust of wind caught the sail of the windmill, breaking his lance and causing him and his mount to take a tremendous pratfall. This scene nearly caused his squire, Sancho Panza, to come unglued with laughter.

BLACK BEAUTY

Black Beauty was written nearly a century ago by the English writer Anna Sewell who loved horses and despised the slobs who mistreated them. She wrote the book to be entertaining, and also to induce kindness and sympathy toward horses, and understanding treatment of them. The book was a roaring success and was instrumental in helping end the plight of mistreated horses. Although Black Beauty had a rough life at times, he was finally sold to a man who loved him, and treated him with much kindness.

"It's Black Beauty!"

PEGASUS

If you were anything but an ancient Greek and saw a flying horse soaring through the sky, you would think you had stopped too long at the Last-Chance Saloon for a few more drinks of fire water than was good for you. The ancient Greeks, however, did tell of a great white stallion with wings, called Pegasus, that was the horse of the gods and goddesses of Mount Olympus. He was the special pet of Apollo, the Sun God, for whom he carried thunder and lightning on his back, some of which would occasionally fall off and cause a bit of a rumpus down below.

Next flight is the same time tomorrow.

BRIGHAM

Brigham was an Indian pony that was a buffalo hunter's dream horse. As the buffalo were such unpredictable beasts and would swerve at any given moment, it made hunting them a dangerous occupation. However, hunting buffalo, to Brigham, was almost second nature and he was able to keep his cool under what would often seem to be impossible situations.

Buffalo Bill bought Brigham from a Ute Indian who had named him after Brigham Young, the leader of the Mormons. Brigham was a raggle-taggle looking horse, but that did not faze Buffalo Bill, who knew Brigham was worth his weight in gold. Buffalo Bill worked for the Kansas Pacific Railway providing buffalo meat for its workers. Needless to say, they ate like royalty. It was because of this wonderful horse that William F. Cody earned the name Buffalo Bill.

Brigham was the horse Partner Buffalo Bill used for the buffalo hunting which earned him his nickname.

OLD STEAMBOAT

A bucking bronco's worth is measured by his meanness and his ability to fight his riders to the bitter end. When Steamboat was a colt some wit said, "He was the most even-tempered horse in the West. He was mad all the time." When the ill-tempered Mr. Steamboat was old enough to be broke, the ranch hands could hardly wait for the big event. The cowboy who can tame that headstrong horse will have to have glue on his pants, they predicted. They were right. Steamboat put up the worst fight ever seen in those parts. It was as if a charge of dynamite had been ignited. He leaped and twisted so hard and fast that in no time at all the rider looked as if he were headed for the moon. He shot off Steamboat's back for a not- too- soft landing on terra firma. The other cowboys tried to ride him but no one could stay on his back. His owner, John Coble, knew he had a winner so he entered him in some rodeo contests. Steamboat took to the work like a glutton to a pie-eating contest. He had a long career, thirteen years to be exact. In all that time only one man, Dick Stanley, managed to stay on him long enough to make an official ride. Steamboat made more than half a million tax-free dollars in gate money.

Old Steamboat was prized for his meanness.

If by chance you
win the grand trophy
there are many
good uses to put it to.

There is nothing
like it for soaking
aching muscles.

It's perfect
for the old
card-in-the-hat game.

It can also be
very utilitarian when
put on the trophy shelf.

**And above all don't forget
to praise the one who helped you win the cup.**